SARATOGA

SARATOGA

George Ranalli

edited by oscar riera ojeda   photography by paul warchol   introduction by michael sorkin

single building series   oro editions

For David Burney and the residents of Saratoga Village

SARATOGA SPRINGS!
BY MICHAEL SORKIN

Why is this little building important? It is George Ranalli's first, fully free-standing, built-from-scratch work. Hard not to regard a development of such signal importance for our architecture, a cause for celebration, an occasion long-awaited and a bit of surprise, given the architect's stature. That we know Ranalli's work so well already, is in part a byproduct of its easy dissemination over the ether. Like a number of his peers, George figures importantly in the architectural firmament because his work is widely published and exceptionally well regarded in a representational culture that simply elides the conceptual and the literal. In the case of Ranalli, the profusion of realized interiors, objects, additions and other products of his supple and lapidary hand have perhaps persuaded us that many of the major works – designs that grow gracefully from a long rich line of his sensibility – are simply *there*.

That so much of this work consists of un-built projects might not be an issue for many, but it is for Ranalli. This is not to say that his production isn't visionary, that it can't teach from the position of the image. Obviously, there are depths to his representations that can explain, argue and intoxicate. For years, Ranalli has been meticulously developing an architectural idiom that is at once singular and connected, rich in detail and spatiality, exquisitely elegant, and ever engaged in the vital intercourse of the social. For many, this is simply architecture, full stop. Is it enough? Not for George, and not for us.

Unlike so much architecture, seemingly designed for the page, Ranalli's work, lives larger in the concrete. It may be that the qualities that sustain and inspire this work are simply out of sync with the immaterial feeling of so much of our contemporary architecture with its uniformity of detail, fetish for non-

orthogonal form, love of transparency, willful defiance of gravity and servility to the most retrograde programs. George Ranalli stands outside this stream of fashion, just as he stands outside the backward-looking branch of the profession that claims thumping its virtuous chest, to be building within some sense of "tradition", in general one that has long been pronounced dead.

Ranalli on the other hand, works in a tradition that retains a principle of development, a living tradition, not one recaptured from the moribund reaches of the architectural past. He continues to research, refine and extend one of the key taxonomic streams of modernity. The architect whose books appear most prominently on Ranalli's shelves is Frank Lloyd Wright and the master is pivotal in the development of his work. The sense of the collusion of space and detail, the richness of elaboration, the intense but disciplined materiality, the feeling for landscape, and the visionary openness to the suggestiveness of context are qualities abundantly shared between them. This is by no means to say that Ranalli is a Wrightian, rather Wright was the giant in a flow of sensibility that both preceded and followed him. His fellow travelers certainly include the Amsterdam School, the Arts and Crafts movement, Otto Wagner, Louis Sullivan, Alvar Aalto, Carlo Scarpa, Le Corbusier and Raimund Abraham amongst many more.

What unites these figures for Ranalli is a set of characteristics that join the spatial, the tectonic and the social. Ranalli's work enjoys one of its many singularities in the way it combines a feeling for flowing space with a more orthodox, even quirky, reverence for the chamber, for spaces isolated in their particularity. The union unique becomes unique because Ranalli does not simply produce a breezy continuity throughout the project but a palpable flow that eddies and laminates and through which the movement of bodies is both straightforward and complex. This architecture abounds in niches and reveals, in projections and articulations, in complex detail, in moments of great intimacy, in a clear sense of the way in which space is social, conducing privacy, intimacy and more public forms of behavior.

George Ranalli is a total architect, one who sees continuity not simply between building and environment, but between building and its inhabitation. A vision that extends to both the inanimate and the lively. One of the great furniture designers of the day, Ranalli sees autonomous objects – tables, chairs, hardware – as a piece of his larger architectural configuring. There is a remarkably genetic quality to Ranalli's tectonics of the small, his ability to establish an utterly persuasive continuity between scales by working at once, from small to large and large to small. In this sense, the work is almost gothic. Just as one understands the logic of the cathedral in the DNA exposed by a cut through a pier, so Ranalli's corbels and echelons signal an architecture that is not simply *sui generis*, but in which a beautiful, completely worked out prosody structures the whole.

The Saratoga Center flanks and extends a particularly homely public housing slab, a typically deracinated example of the modernist tower. The new building manages – on an amazingly low budget – both to interrogate the slab as a resistant autonomous entity and to reconsider its spare and constricted vocabulary from a formal viewpoint. The adjoining tower is virtually starved of detail and what there is oppresses in its crudeness, the visible lack of concern by its designers to do anything but minimize costs and character. It embeds a semi-punitive message that has long affected public projects for the poor, a kind of grudging insistence on an idea of the minimum that clearly suggests that any artistic supplement to the basic necessities of inhabitation is more generous than the culture wishes to be.

Ranalli's building is a stunning rebuke to all that, but done in a way that does not simply condemn its context, but seeks to reclaim it for a better, more civic idea of community building. Where the slab has generic metal sash, Saratoga has exquisite mahogany windows. Where the slab has homely buff brick, crudely laid up in unvarying courses, Saratoga has bricks of luminous orange and Roman proportion, beautifully articulated and trimmed with GFRC elements of musical richness. Where the slab and its interior are utterly resistant to detail and irregularity, Saratoga fascinates with amazing shifts in proportion and rhythm, with a panoply of beautiful elements – from cast stone scuppers, to steel kick moldings – that give the whole an almost palatial feel.

This sense of civic grandeur is no place more evident than in the building's main event, its "community room." This is surely one of the most elegant

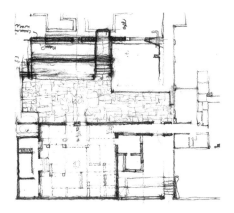

spaces in the city, worked out with precision and joy. From the beautifully articulated ceiling and floating roof, with their wonderfully rich penetrations, directionality and sense of flight, to the sensuous concrete wainscoting, the complex and rich interplay of natural and artificial illumination and the lovely parquet on the floor, the room is not only a superb site for communal celebration, but a clear cause for one. This is an elevating space, so far from the reclaimed church basement or gym that typically serves for the kinds of gatherings it will soon support.

The siting of the building and the articulation of the spaces around its perimeter are also remarkably urbane. Saratoga sits with great conviction on the street and links the slab on one side with an existing commercial building on the other, to form an ensemble that feels completely natural. Rather than diminishing its neighbors by creating a sense of anomalous quality, Saratoga enhances them by sharing the authority of its articulation generously. This is the result both of the way Saratoga works within a familiar universe of materiality and proportion and the way in which it is the fulcrum for the reorganization of the irregular block on which it sits with its neighbors. Ranalli rearticulates the conditions of entry to the slab and gives its displacement from the street, an urban logic it did not previously possess.

This is a particular revelation. Ranalli has brought the slab into a truly singular and complex relationship with its extended context that yields a fascinating hybrid. No longer enslaved by the tower-in-the-park *parti*, the slab becomes part of an articulated perimeter that both holds the street and opens up into a series of small public spaces. These modulate access and provide useful intermediaries between the buildings and the street, a group of small outdoor public rooms. The ensemble has a clear front and back, two very different

conditions that inspire very different responses. If the main street conditions are relatively opaque, around the back, where the scheme opens to a large courtyard that extends across the site to the street in the rear, the project is more transparent, more permeable, more continuous with its protected social and spatial extension, held within the calm embrace of the "L" it forms with the slab. Here, Ranalli has organized a larger, more protected social site, a soft piazza.

The success of this building clearly derives not simply from the masterful articulation of its form and program, but from its author's passionate sense of a wider physical and social context. Visiting the building at several stages of its construction, I've made the drive to Brownsville with George along several different routes and we've roamed the neighborhood together. These journeys have provided a fine reminder of Ranalli's wonderful view, his way of seeing the city, the nesting of his architectural vision in the urban and the political. Ranalli identifies powerfully with a civic tradition in which public works are meant to represent the highest forms of cultural aspiration. He is forever pointing out beautiful schools and firehouses, built a century ago from which a spirit of public pride radiates from their strong and substantial forms, buildings that speak volumes about a progressive public project to elevate the character of daily life.

Ranalli clearly sees his own project as one restoring this sense of consequence to the public realm. Within a few blocks of Saratoga, he finds the elements of the spatial and social ensemble that he so tenaciously identifies with the urban good. The beautiful schools and churches of a century ago are embedded in a traditional architectural field of row house blocks and public parks, a pattern so coarsely interrupted by the oppressive clarities of the city of slabs. Ranalli also clearly sees the communal importance of the great private spaces of public gathering of those days and we've cruised nearby Broadway, once home to bustling crowds and a series of great movie palaces, celebrations of assembly, of a sense of the shared enterprise of citizenship, of belonging.

Part of the brilliance of Saratoga is the way in which this sense of the consequence of civic construction is re-inscribed in a normative pattern that sought to annihilate its predecessor. What Ranalli recognizes in his own singular way, is that the structure of human relations and values he identifies with the good city can be produced with a variety of architectures, if they are able to successfully embody long-standing institutions, spatialities of connectedness and gathering, and if they insist on the consequentiality of pride and of hope. In a language of bright originality, Saratoga incorporates a long and deep tradition of gathering and purpose, a sense of the centeredness of community and a heroic insistence on the idea of beauty in service.

Both the dilemma and the triumph of Saratoga are reflected in a sense of surprise, bordering on wonderment by many who live in the adjoining project that they have been given *that kind of a building*. Here is the representation of our sad culture, of diminished collective expectations alongside a truly stunning riposte. On a humble site in a poor neighborhood, in an "outer" borough, George Ranalli has overcome a raft of taxing bureaucratic and financial obstacles to produce – for people persuaded that *they don't deserve it* – a gem, a great work of architecture, a space of hope and happiness, an affirmation of the possibility that urban life can be good for all of us.

Michael Sorkin is the Director of the Graduate Urban Design Program at the City College of New York. From 1993 to 2000 he was Professor of Urbanism and Director of the Institute of Urbanism at the Academy of Fine Arts in Vienna. Previously, Sorkin has been a professor at numerous schools of architecture including the Architectural Association, Cooper Union (for ten years), Columbia, Yale (holding both Davenport and Bishop Chairs), Harvard, Cornell (Gensler Chair), Nebraska (Hyde Chair), Illinois, Pennsylvania, Texas, Michigan (Saarinen Chair) and Minnesota. Between 2005 - 2006, Sorkin was directing studio projects for the post-Katrina reconstruction of Biloxi and New Orleans. Sorkin lectures widely and is the author of many articles in a wide range of both professional and general publications. Currently, he is contributing editor for *Architectural Record and Metropolis*.

For ten years, he was the architecture critic of *The Village Voice*. His books include *Variations on A Theme Park, Exquisite Corpse, Local Code, Giving Ground* (edited with Joan Copjec), *Wiggle* (a monograph of the studio's work), *Some Assembly Required, Other Plans, The Next Jerusalem, After The Trade Center* (edited with Sharon Zukin), *Starting From Zero, Analyzing Ambasz, Against the Wall, Twenty Minutes in Manhattan, Work on the City, All Over the Map, and Indefensible Space*.

SARATOGA COMMUNITY CENTER
940 HANCOCK STREET
BROOKLYN, NEW YORK 11233
2008

In projects ranging from doorknobs to residences and office buildings, George Ranalli experiments with a distinctive brand of ornamentation, a machine-cut, linear vocabulary that suggests computer age manufacturing processes and geometries. For New York City's public housing agency, he uses glass-fiber-reinforced-concrete (GFRC) lintels and copestones and buff-grey cement panels, with routed joints indoors, to imbue a new community center, with layers of meaning and visual interest. The 5,000-square-foot facility is set on the plaza of a typical 1960's super block, next to an 18-story mixed income housing slab. It expands the program of city-sponsored recreation by linking it to an existing recreational center on the tower's first floor with a long hall, perforated by doors and windows. New facilities include, a large multipurpose community room, a game room, a reading room, offices, kitchen and bathrooms. Ranalli's plan wisely connects new landscaped areas to existing socializing spaces, such as a small sitting area, but he encloses the plaza with the center's bulk. The result gives the largely Hispanic and African-American residents a safer, more social open space. The over all effect of the new structures is a unifying, layered gesture. The center's ochre iron-spot thin brick and limestone base, blend with the neighborhood palette and the engaging GFRC accents readily identify entries. Each façade is unique; steel and mahogany-framed clerestory rises above the variously stepped masonry. The idiosyncratic ornamentation offers a specific formal articulation, but the perceived effect is universal and timeless – a sort of visual Esperanto and a suitably pluralist gesture for a lasting public presence among diverse local users.

C.C. Sullivan, Editor
ARCHITECTURE Magazine, February 2004

above saratoga early sketch section

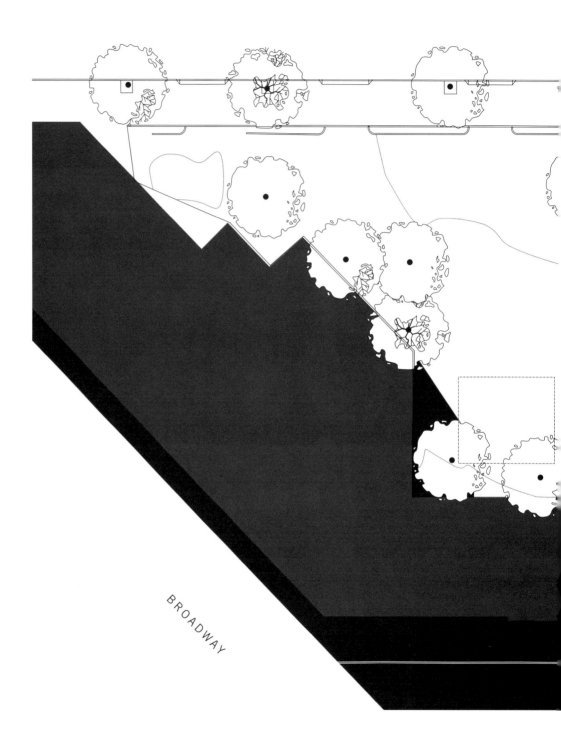

BROADWAY

SARATOGA AVENUE

HANCOCK STREET

site plan

1   community room (multi-purpose)
2   director's office
3   assistant director's office
4   entry court
5   existing court
6   game room (multi-purpose)
7   reading room
8   entry for existing building
9   new courtyard
10 overlook
11 existing courtyard
12 cinema screen

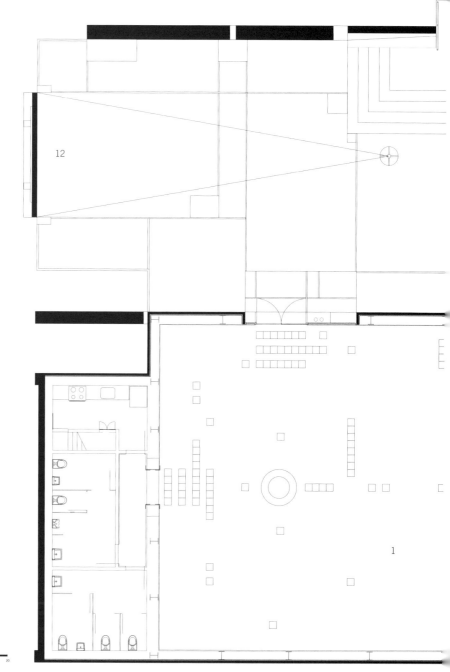

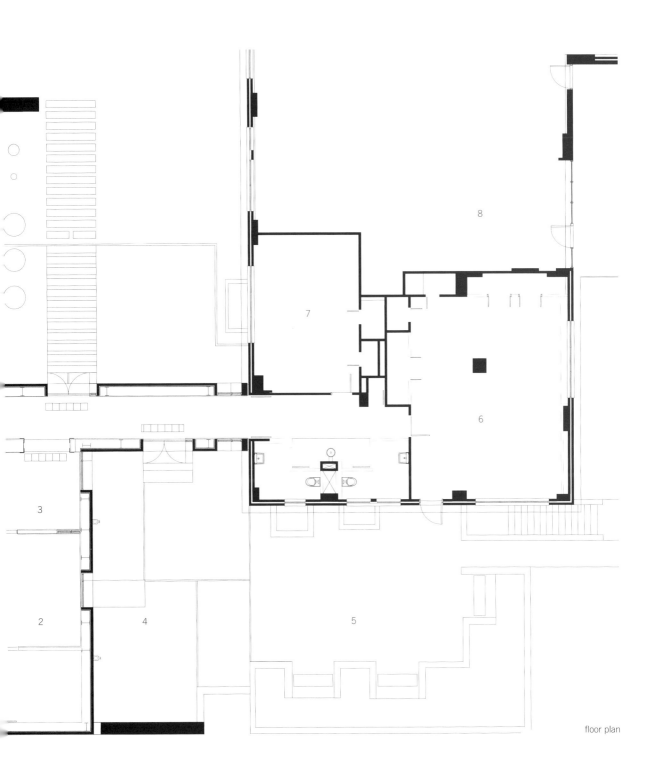

floor plan

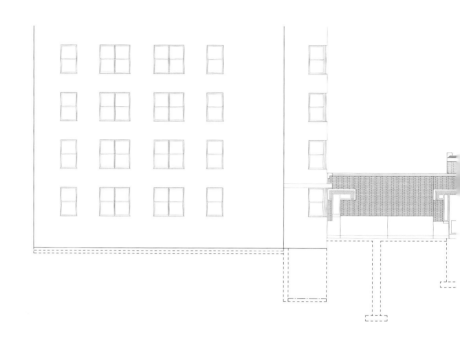

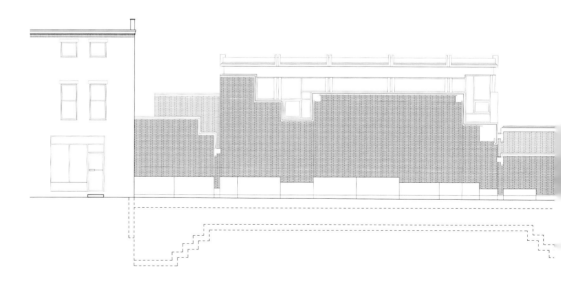

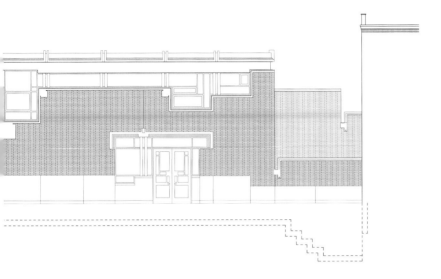

south elevation

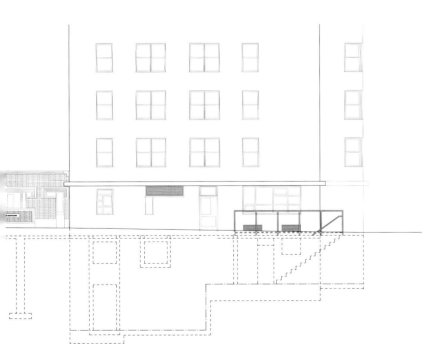

north elevation

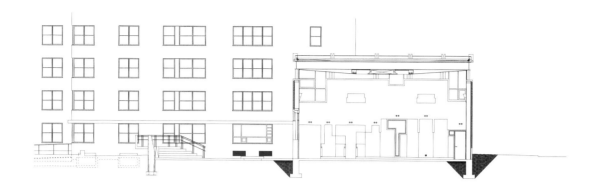

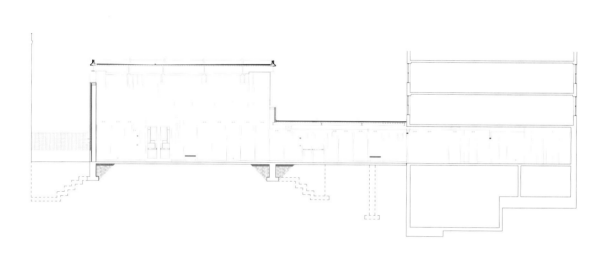

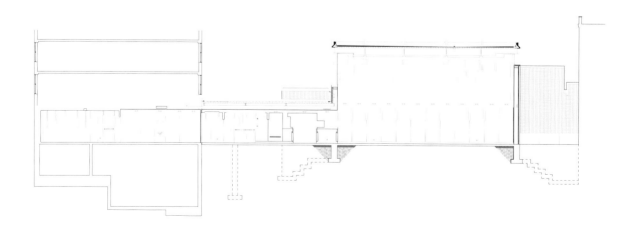

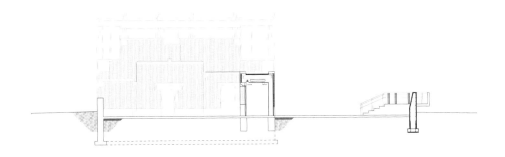

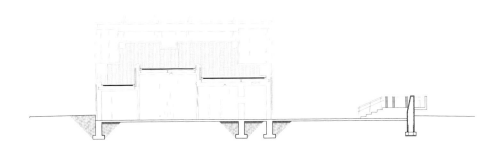

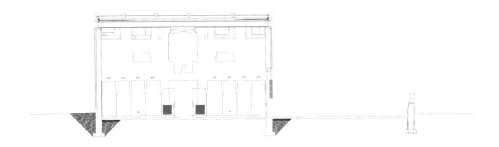

sections

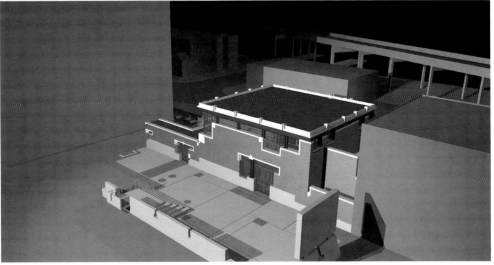

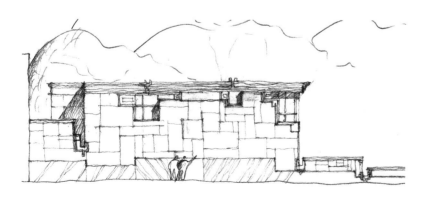

left to right aerial view. above sketch of the new
saratoga community center.

right hancock street entry view.

previous spread entry courtyard. top detail view of the director's office window. limestone blocks are at the bottom, elongated iron spot roman brick above and gfrc lintel. clearly visible on the interior is the window from the director's office into the main assembly room. bottom detail view lintel over the director's office window. right view of the director's office wall.

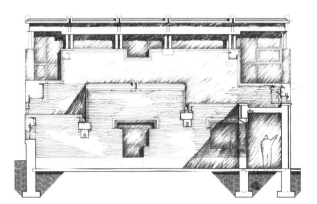

left detail view of the assistant director's window and spaces beyond. top view along the courtyard entry doors looking at the assistant director's office. bottom saratoga early sketch.

following spread view of the director's office coping cap and the cornice and structure of the main assembly room.

above detail view along the hancock street elevation of the building. right view of the corner of the director's office and the main assembly room beyond.

SARATOGA VILLAGE COMMUNITY CENTER

left detail of the low courtyard wall with the name of the center in the foreground and the storage room block just behind it. top detail of the entry wall on hancock street.

bottom detail of the wall fragment between the entry doors and the small window in the hall connecting the new center to the existing center in the slab building.

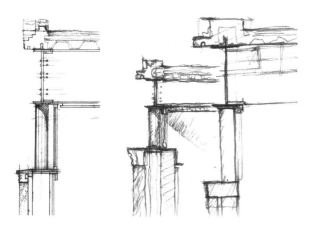

top detail of the scupper, director's office block
and the upper structure of the main assembly
room. bottom early sketch of structure.

right scupper detail on the street side elevation.
scupper from the director's office roof beyond.

left hancock sreet elevation. top view on hancock street from the back of the building. bottom elevation sketch of building from hancock street.

following spread main garden elevation. the existing 16 story saratoga houses building is on the left.

above detail of the garden entry and elevation
looking toward the large door and window.

right corner detail of scupper, gfrc stone work,
elongated iron spot roman brick and mahogany
window above.

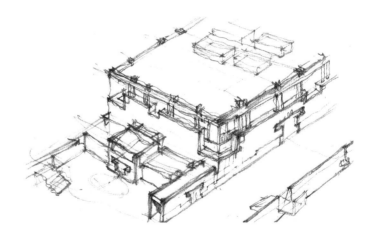

left view of the large garden door and window. top full view of the garden elevation looking toward the existing 16 story slab building. bottom saratoga early sketch.

top view looking up at the rear corner of the building. bottom detail view of the rear wall of the building featuring the gfrc cornice on top of the steel beam.

right detail of the garden wall elevation where it meets with an existing building. following spread detail of the entry doors on the garden side of the building.

previous spread garden elevation of the community center. the main entry doors are on the left side in the connector between the existing center and the new addition and the main assembly room can be seen as the large block with the roof supported by paired steel columns. top segment of the garden elevation of the building. this view illustrates the large window-door configuration from the main assembly space, the upper window, the paired columns supporting the roof and the gfrc cornice. bottom a sketch of the garden elevation of the building. right detail of the large mahogany entry door looking through into the large room. following spread interior view looking toward garden entry.

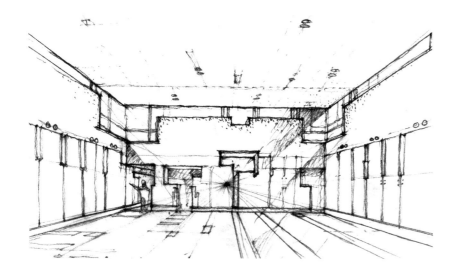

previous spread full view of the main assembly
room looking toward the entry. above and right
view of the main assembly room looking toward
the director's office.

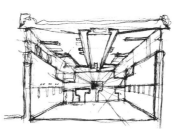 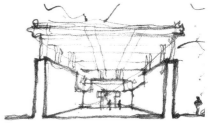

left view of the main assembly space from the entry hall. from this view you can see the shaped and sculpted ceiling with the variable lighting design. top view looking at the rear wall of the main assembly space and entrance to the bathrooms and service kitchen. sculptural shapes on the wall conceal mechanical and lighting equipment. inlay floor pattern echos the composition of the room. bottom sketches early sketches of main assembly room.

above view at the entrance looking left into the assembly room. on the left is the window from the director's office into the main assembly room. clearly visible is the decorative pattern in the wood floor. wall beyond has plycem cement panels screw assembled to the plaster wall behind. right wall detail in the main assembly room. lacquer coated plycem cement panels are screw assembled to the plaster wall beyond.

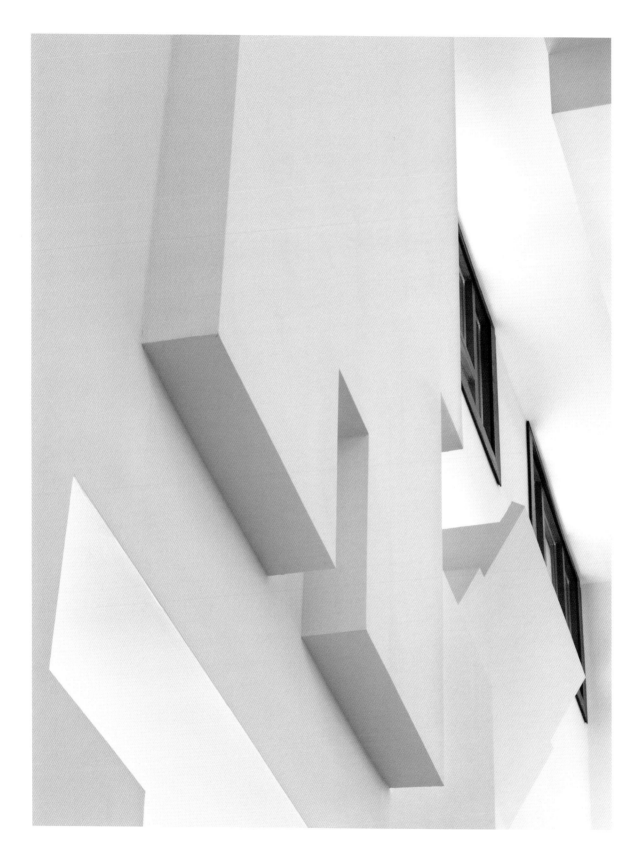

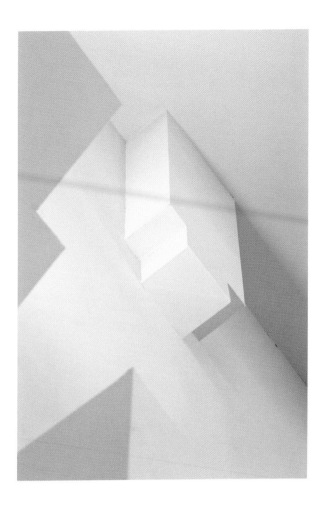

left view looking up at the back wall of the main space. plaster sculptural forms of the mechanical ductwork enclosure, the wall light sconce beyond and the upper mahogany windows.

above view looking up in the main room. plaster detail of the roof water drain enclosure. following spread view looking up at the shaped ceiling.

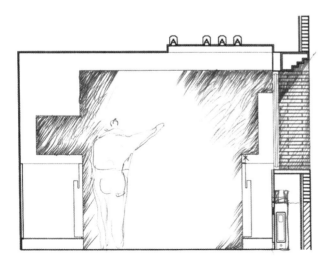

ASSISTANT
DIRECTORS
OFFICE

left view of the entry hall of the building. the assistant director's office is on the left and the main assembly room is beyond. left bottom early sketch of assistant director's office.

above view from the entry hall into the assistant director's office, reception area and the director's office beyond. pictured in the office is a custom designed desk.

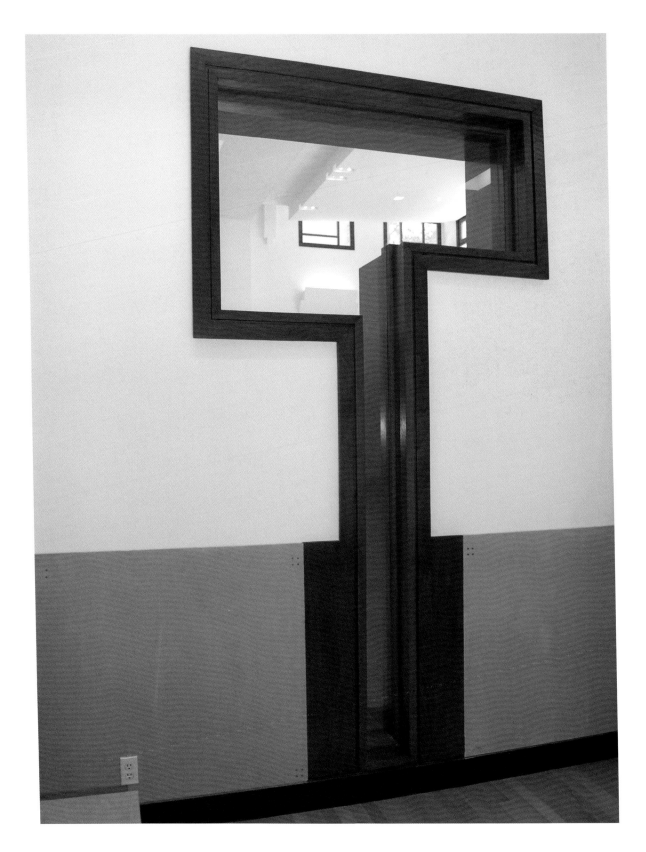

left detail view inside the director's office looking at the mahogany window into the main assembly room.

above director's office with custom designed desk and window into the main assembly room on the right.

left detail of the wall panels of the main assembly room at the entry into the assistant director's office and reception area.

above detail view from the assistant director's office into the main assembly room. following spread dusk view of the garden elevation.

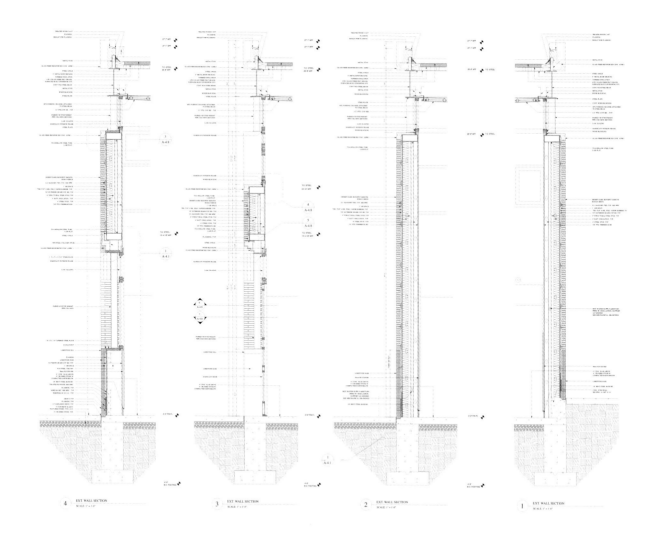

4   EXT. WALL SECTION
    SCALE 1" = 1'-0"

3   EXT. WALL SECTION
    SCALE 1" = 1'-0"

2   EXT. WALL SECTION
    SCALE 1" = 1'-0"

1   EXT. WALL SECTION
    SCALE 1" = 1'-0"

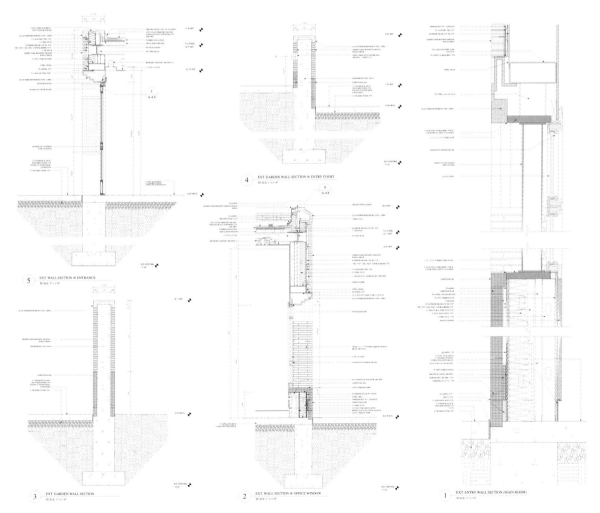

4   EXT. GARDEN WALL SECTION @ ENTRY COURT
      SCALE: 1" = 1'-0"

5   EXT. WALL SECTION @ ENTRANCE
      SCALE: 1" = 1'-0"

3   EXT. GARDEN WALL SECTION
      SCALE: 1" = 1'-0"

2   EXT. WALL SECTION @ OFFICE WINDOW
      SCALE: 1" = 1'-0"

1   EXT. ENTRY WALL SECTION (MAIN ROOM)
      SCALE: 1" = 1'-0"

wall sections

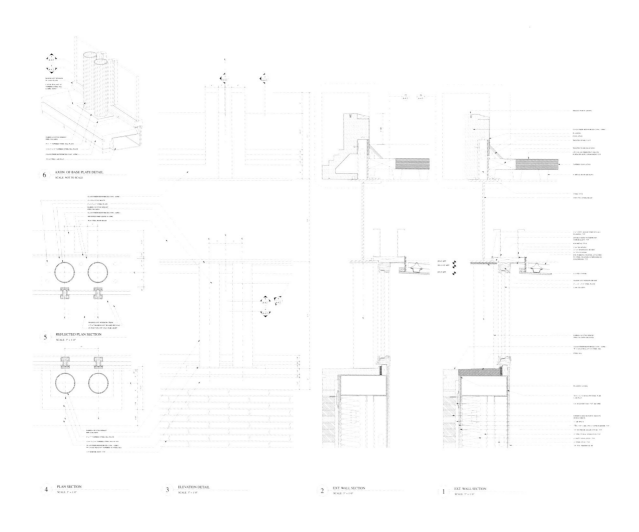

6 AXON. OF BASE PLATE DETAIL
SCALE: NOT TO SCALE

5 REFLECTED PLAN SECTION
SCALE: 1" = 1-0"

4 PLAN SECTION
SCALE: 3" = 1-0"

3 ELEVATION DETAIL
SCALE: 3" = 1-0"

2 EXT. WALL SECTION
SCALE: 3" = 1-0"

1 EXT. WALL SECTION
SCALE: 3" = 1-0"

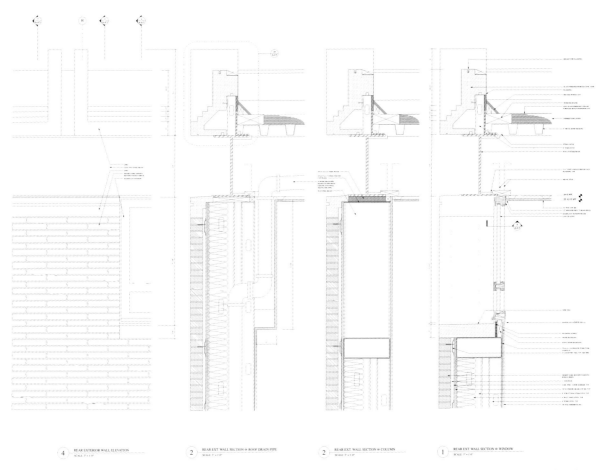

4 REAR EXTERIOR WALL ELEVATION
SCALE: 3" = 1'-0"

2 REAR EXT. WALL SECTION @ ROOF DRAIN PIPE
SCALE: 3" = 1'-0"

2 REAR EXT. WALL SECTION @ COLUMN
SCALE: 3" = 1'-0"

1 REAR EXT. WALL SECTION @ WINDOW
SCALE: 3" = 1'-0"

upper wall sections

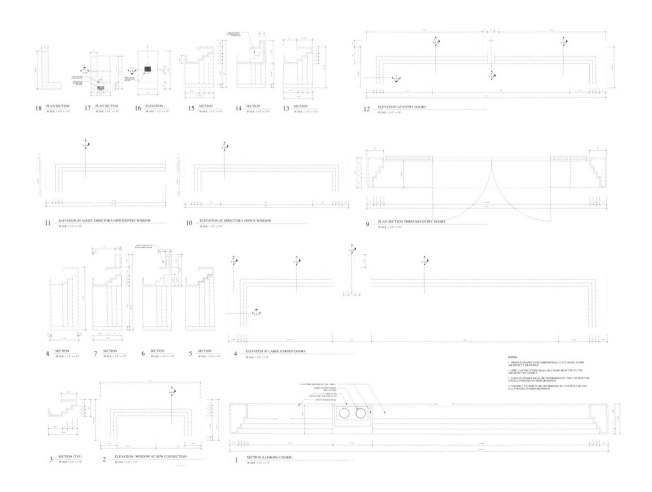

18 PLAN SECTION
    SCALE: 1 1/2" = 1'-0"

17 PLAN SECTION
    SCALE: 1 1/2" = 1'-0"

16 ELEVATION
    SCALE: 1 1/2" = 1'-0"

15 SECTION
    SCALE: 1 1/2" = 1'-0"

14 SECTION
    SCALE: 1 1/2" = 1'-0"

13 SECTION
    SCALE: 1 1/2" = 1'-0"

12 ELEVATION AT ENTRY DOORS
    SCALE: 1 1/2" = 1'-0"

11 ELEVATION AT ASSIST. DIRECTOR'S OFFICE/ENTRY WINDOW
    SCALE: 1 1/2" = 1'-0"

10 ELEVATION AT DIRECTOR'S OFFICE WINDOW
    SCALE: 1 1/2" = 1'-0"

9   PLAN SECTION THROUGH ENTRY DOORS
    SCALE: 1 1/2" = 1'-0"

8   SECTION
    SCALE: 1 1/2" = 1'-0"

7   SECTION
    SCALE: 1 1/2" = 1'-0"

6   SECTION
    SCALE: 1 1/2" = 1'-0"

5   SECTION
    SCALE: 1 1/2" = 1'-0"

4   ELEVATION AT LARGE GARDEN DOORS
    SCALE: 1 1/2" = 1'-0"

3   SECTION (TYP.)
    SCALE: 1 1/2" = 1'-0"

2   ELEVATION- WINDOW AT NEW CONNECTION
    SCALE: 1 1/2" = 1'-0"

1   SECTION (LOOKING UNDER)
    SCALE: 1 1/2" = 1'-0"

NOTES:

1. PROFILE SHAPES TO BE DIMENSIONALLY ACCURATE AS PER ARCHITECT'S DRAWINGS.

2. GFRC CASTING STONE SHALL BE COLOR SELECTED BY THE ARCHITECT BY SAMPLE.

3. VOIDS IN STONES SHALL BE DETERMINED BY THE CONTRACTOR AND ILLUSTRATED IN SHOP DRAWINGS.

4. CONSTRUCTION SYSTEM TO BE DETERMINED BY CONTRACTOR AND ILLUSTRATED IN SHOP DRAWINGS.

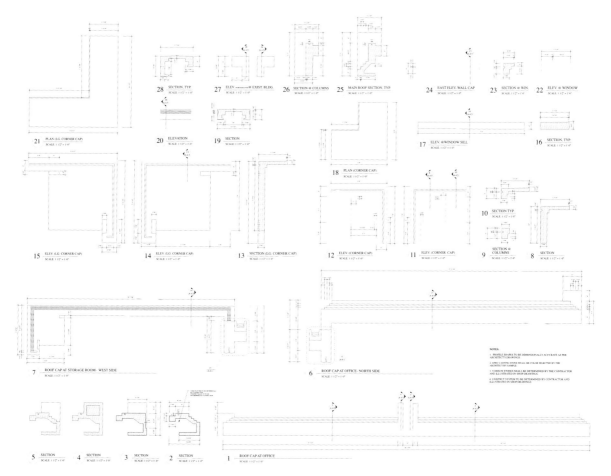

28 SECTION, TYP.
SCALE: 1 1/2" = 1'-0"

27 ELEV. PARTIAL CTR @ EXIST. BLDG.
SCALE: 1 1/2" = 1'-0"

26 SECTION @ COLUMNS
SCALE: 1 1/2" = 1'-0"

25 MAIN ROOF SECTION, TYP.
SCALE: 1 1/2" = 1'-0"

24 EAST ELEV. WALL CAP
SCALE: 1 1/2" = 1'-0"

23 SECTION @ WIN.
SCALE: 1 1/2" = 1'-0"

22 ELEV. @ WINDOW
SCALE: 1 1/2" = 1'-0"

21 PLAN (LG. CORNER CAP)

20 ELEVATION
SCALE: 1 1/2" = 1'-0"

19 SECTION
SCALE: 1 1/2" = 1'-0"

17 ELEV. @ WINDOW SILL
SCALE: 1 1/2" = 1'-0"

16 SECTION, TYP.
SCALE: 1 1/2" = 1'-0"

18 PLAN (CORNER CAP)
SCALE: 1 1/2" = 1'-0"

15 ELEV. (LG. CORNER CAP)
SCALE: 1 1/2" = 1'-0"

14 ELEV. (LG. CORNER CAP)
SCALE: 1 1/2" = 1'-0"

13 SECTION (LG. CORNER CAP)
SCALE: 1 1/2" = 1'-0"

12 ELEV. (CORNER CAP)
SCALE: 1 1/2" = 1'-0"

11 ELEV. (CORNER CAP)
SCALE: 1 1/2" = 1'-0"

10 SECTION TYP.
SCALE: 1 1/2" = 1'-0"

9 SECTION @ COLUMNS
SCALE: 1 1/2" = 1'-0"

8 SECTION
SCALE: 1 1/2" = 1'-0"

7 ROOF CAP AT STORAGE ROOM- WEST SIDE
SCALE: 1 1/2" = 1'-0"

6 ROOF CAP AT OFFICE- NORTH SIDE
SCALE: 1 1/2" = 1'-0"

NOTES:
1. PROFILE SHAPES TO BE DIMENSIONALLY ACCURATE AS PER ARCHITECT'S DRAWINGS.
2. GFRC CASTING STONE SHALL BE COLOR SELECTED BY THE ARCHITECT BY SAMPLE.
3. VOIDS IN STONES SHALL BE DETERMINED BY THE CONTRACTOR AND ILLUSTRATED IN SHOP DRAWINGS.
4. UNISTRUT SYSTEM TO BE DETERMINED BY CONTRACTOR AND ILLUSTRATED IN SHOP DRAWINGS.

5 SECTION
SCALE: 1 1/2" = 1'-0"

4 SECTION
SCALE: 1 1/2" = 1'-0"

3 SECTION
SCALE: 1 1/2" = 1'-0"

2 SECTION
SCALE: 1 1/2" = 1'-0"

1 ROOF CAP AT OFFICE
SCALE: 1 1/2" = 1'-0"

grfc details

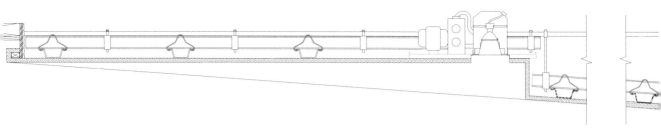

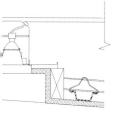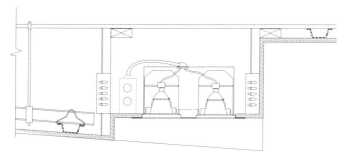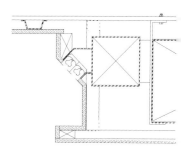

ceiling section

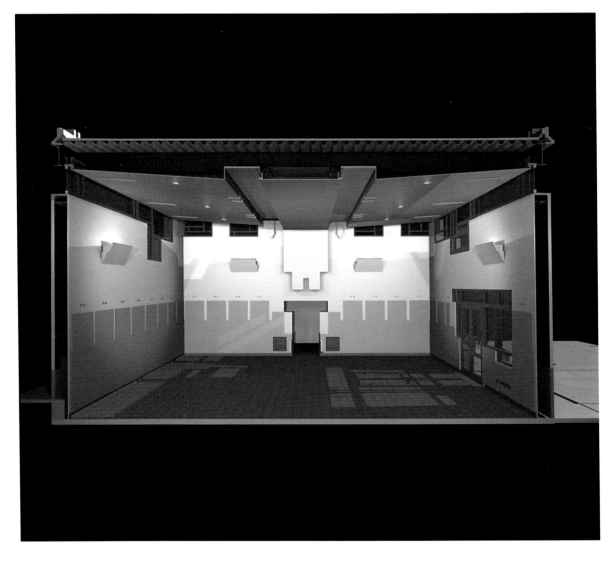

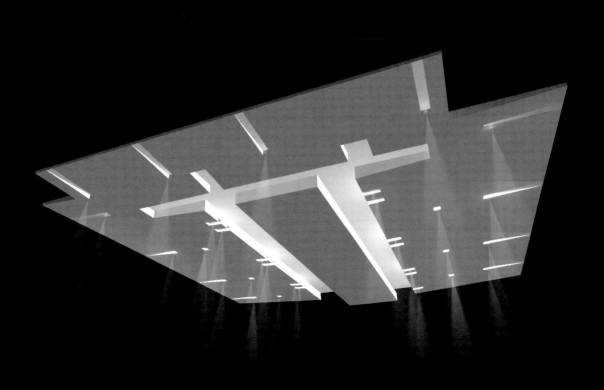

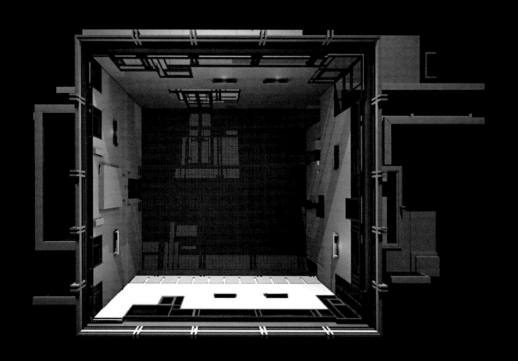

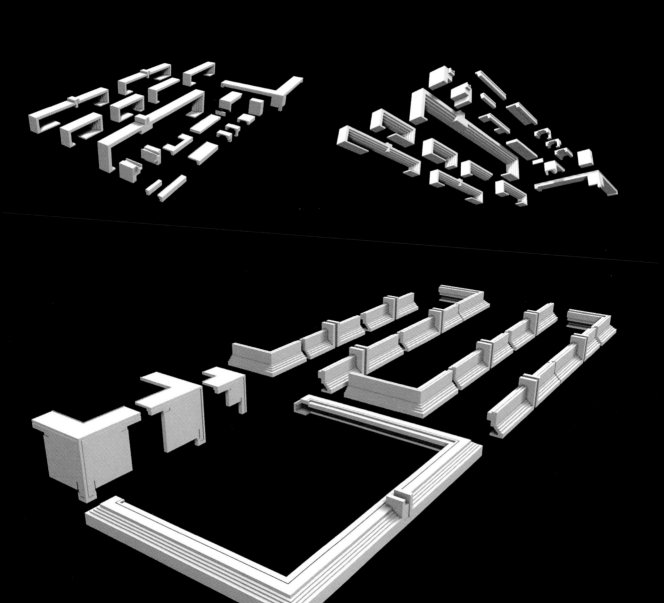
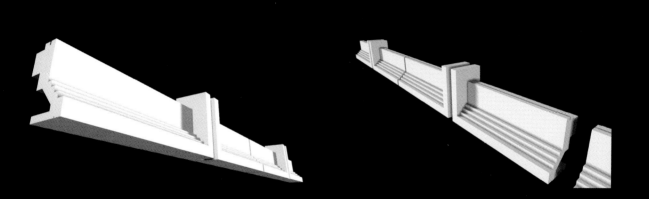

Project Name	Renovation & addition, Saratoga Avenue Community Center
Location	Brooklyn, New York, USA
Building Size	5,500 sq.ft. new building; 1,500 sq.ft. renovation existing interior
Completion	2008
Owner	The New York City Housing Authority The City of New York David Burney, Director of Design
Architect	George Ranalli, Architect New York, NY, USA
Project Team	George Ranalli; Principal & Designer Mario Gentile; Project Architect Hollace Metzger, Hayden Marrero; Additional Project Architects Olivier Calderari, Brock Danner, Price Harrison, Fran Leadon; Assistants
Project Consultants	Robert Silman, Structural Engineer George Langer, Mechanical Engineer Stephen Falk, Specifications/Construction Consultant Joseph DiBernardo, Hillman-DiBernardo, Lighting Consultants
Contractor	Master General Contractors, Long Island City, N.Y.
Aerial Photographs	Julian Olivas
Portrait of George Ranalli	Sofia Ranalli

Photographer Paul Warchol was born in New Jersey in 1954. He attended the Cooper Union School of Art where he received a BFA (Bachelor of Fine Arts, degree). He has been photographing architecture since 1978 and continues to be featured in architectural publications worldwide. Recently, his photos have been the focus of a series of 8 books on architecture and design, edited by Silvio San Pietro and Matteo Cercelloni with the Italian Publisher Edizioni l'Archivolto. In 1998, he collaborated with Mayer Rus, then editor of Interior Design magazine, and Monacelli Press to produce *Loft*, a definitive volume on the phenomenon of industrial living space in New York. Paul's work was exhibited in 1995 at Avery Hall, Columbia University in New York and in 1996 was the subject of an exhibition entitled, 'A Recent View of Architecture' at the National Building Museum in Washington DC. He received the AIA Honor Award for Excellence in the field of Architectural Photography in 1996. He and his wife Ursula operate a studio and archive in lower Manhattan.

Paul Warchol Paul Warchol Photography Inc.
224 Centre Street, 5th Floor
New York, New York, 10013
Telephone: 212.431.3461
Facsimile: 212.274.1953
www.warcholphotography.com

Editor Oscar Riera Ojeda is an editor and designer based in Philadelphia and New York. Born in Buenos Aires, Argentina in 1966, he moved to the United States in 1990. Since that time, Riera Ojeda has completed more than 150 books, working with publishers ORO *editions*, Birkhäuser, Byggförlaget, the Monacelli Press, Gustavo Gili, Thames & Hudson, Rizzoli, Whitney Library of Design, Taschen, Images, Rockport, and Kliczkowski. Riera Ojeda is also the creator of several series of architectural books including Architecture in Detail, Art and Architecture, Contemporary World Architects, Ten Houses, The New American Apartment, and The New American House. He is vice director of the Spanish magazine *Casas Internacional* and contributor to numerous publications and newspapers in the field.

The office of **George Ranalli, Architect** opened in 1977 in New York City. Currently the office is located in the Garment District in Manhattan. Over the last 30 years, George Ranalli has worked on projects such as large-scale urban designs, houses in the landscape, additions, renovations, restorations of major landmark buildings, and new constructions in New York, and other states in the U.S. as well as international projects.

George Ranalli is internationally celebrated and published for working in Historic settings or National Register Historic Landmark Buildings, and in environments with rich design and craft traditions. George Ranalli is able to design new buildings and additions to complexes that are contemporary and innovative, while blending seamlessly with the historic mileau.

The projects have developed a rich craft and design vocabulary tied to the origins and roots of an older craft tradition in design and architecture.

George Ranalli is currently the Dean of the School of Architecture, Urban Design and Landscape Architecture at the City College of New York.

George Ranalli, Architect

150 West 28th Street
New York, NY 10001
USA

T: 212.255.6263
F: 212.255.1049

www.georgeranalli.com

ORO *editions*
Publishers of Architecture, Art, and Design
Gordon Goff – Publisher
USA: PO Box 150338, San Rafael, CA 94915 USA
Asia: Block 8, Lorong Bakar Batu #02-04 Singapore 348743
www.oroeditions.com
info@oroeditions.com

Copyright © 2009 by ORO *editions*

ISBN: 978-0-9814628-8-2

Graphic Design: Oscar Riera Ojeda and Davina Tjandra
Copy Editing: Tahzeeb Doctor
Production: Gordon Goff, Joanne Tan, Davina Tjandra
Color Separation and Printing: ORO *editions* Pte Ltd
Covers: 4mm gray boards with debos tip-ons
End Paper Sheets: 150 gsm woodfree paper
Text Paper: 157 gsm premium matt art paper; an off-line gloss spot varnish was applied to all photographs

Distribution

In North America:
Publishers Group West
1700 Fourth Street
Berkeley, CA 94710
USA

In UK and Europe:
John Rule Sales & Marketing
40 Voltaire Road
London SW4 6DH
United Kingdom

In Asia:
Page One Publishing Private Ltd.
20 Kaki Bukit View
Kaki Bukit Techpark II, 415967
Singapore